GW00729054

Did

CRO...

A MISCELLANY

Compiled by Julia Skinner

With particular reference to the work of Martin Andrew

THE FRANCIS FRITH COLLECTION

www.francisfrith.com

Based on a book first published in the United Kingdom in 2006 by The Francis Frith Collection®

This edition published exclusively for Oakridge in 2009 ISBN 978-1-84589-443-6

British Library Cataloguing in Publication Data

Did You Know? Croydon - A Miscellany
Compiled by Julia Skinner
With particular reference to the work of Martin Andrew

The Francis Frith Collection
Frith's Barn, Teffont,
Salisbury, Wiltshire SP3 5QP
Tel: +44 (0) 1722 716 376
Email: info@francisfrith.co.uk
www.francisfrith.com

Printed and bound in Singapore

Front Cover: **CROYDON, SURREY STREET MARKET c1955** C201094p

The colour-tinting is for illustrative purposes only, and is not intended to be historically accurate

CONTENTS

INTRODUCTION

To many people Croydon is a modern town, a forest of tall office blocks intersected by dual carriageways, flyovers and underpasses: a town redeveloped with scant regard for its history. Croydon had greatly expanded in the 19th century, after the coming of the railways in 1839, which had given the town some excellent Victorian architecture. Much of this 19th-century architectural heritage was swept away after the Corporation Act of 1956, in a programme combining new road networks, infrastructure and commercial and public buildings at the height of the era when sweeping away the old 'outdated' buildings of historic towns and cities was seen as the only path for regeneration. The pride of Croydon's councillors, planners, highway engineers and businessmen in their new 'modern' town is reflected in many of the photographs in this book, which were originally taken by the Frith photographers for production as postcards of the exciting new developments.

Croydon has been the butt of many jokes aimed at the enthusiastic approach that was taken in the town to the modernisation of the later half of the 20th century; at one time the term 'Croydonisation' was used to describe any town landscape in the country that was being changed by tower blocks of offices and relentless road systems. Croydon is often mocked for its supposed lack of culture and its suburban atmosphere, but this attitude is unfair to the Croydon of the 21st century, which boasts several high-quality arts venues, foremost amongst which is the Fairfield Halls, the home of the London Mozart Players, the UK's longest-established chamber orchestra, whose Principal Guest Conductor is flautist Sir James Galway.

Despite all the change that Croydon has experienced, the fundamentals of a town prove more difficult to destroy. Surprisingly to some, there are still some buildings of historic significance and outstanding importance surviving in Croydon, including an archbishop's medieval palace, a medieval parish church and a Tudor

hospital, or almshouses. The main streets of the town follow a pattern established by the Middle Ages, which is still discernible. There is a large triangular market place with the High Street forming its east side; on the west side of the market place is Surrey Street, where the street market still takes place. Since medieval times, the centre of the market place has been encroached upon in the well-known process whereby temporary market stalls were replaced by more modern buildings, and in the late 19th century much of the town was redeveloped and improved, so modern development in Croydon is in line with a long tradition of change.

The story of Croydon is full of fascinating characters and events, of which this book can only provide a brief glimpse.

CROYDON AIRPORT FROM THE AIR 1939 AF60370

CROYDON AIRPORT

Croydon Airfield was created during the First World War to provide protection against Zeppelins. It became Britain's chief international airport in 1920, and throughout the inter-war years was virtually the only airport handling international traffic; Imperial Airways, which concentrated on developing long-distance overseas routes, was based initially at Croydon. The airport eventually became too small to cope with the increasing volume of air traffic, and the last passenger flight left Croydon Airport on 30 October 1959; the airport terminal has now been restored, and the Croydon Airport Visitor Centre was opened in October 2000 to tell the story of those golden days of commercial aviation.

Many of the world's pioneer aviators used Croydon Airport in its heyday in the 1920s and 1930s. One of these was the Australian navigator 'Bert' Hinkler, who made the first solo flight from Britain to Australia in 1928. He set off on his historic journey from Croydon on 7 February, and landed in Darwin on 22 February, after flying his two-seat Avro 581E Avian biplane over 11,250 miles in fifteen and a half days.

One of the exhibits in the Croydon Airport Visitor Centre is the flight bag of Britain's pioneering aviation heroine Amy Johnson. She became the first female pilot to fly solo from Britain to Australia, at the age of 26, in 1930. She began the historic flight in her de Havilland DH60 Gipsy Moth G-AAAH from Croydon Airport on 5 May 1930. She landed at Port Darwin, on the northern tip of Australia, nineteen days later, after a dangerous and eventful trip. Amy became a national heroine, and thousands of people came to cheer her on her arrival back at Croydon. A reporter on the Wallington and Carshalton Times wrote: 'Visitors to London have made a special journey to Croydon. Northern dialects mingle with the Cockney accent. And, of course, Croydonians are assembling in their hundreds accompanied by large contingents from Purley, Wallington, Carshalton, Sutton and Cheam … the public enclosure at Plough Lane is filled with thousands of people, all struggling for a good view-point. In Sandy Lane and Foresters Row there are 4,000 cars parked, while the whole length of the Purley Way is filled with humans all cheerfully facing a three-hour wait for their heroine'.

HAUNTED CROYDON

The Wheatsheaf Inn in Thornton Heath was the subject of investigation by a team from Paranormal Investigations UK in 2004, after the landlady, Mrs Maria Seal, had reported some mysterious occurrences, including bottles moving on the bar and a permanently cold boiler room. Mrs Seal believed that the pub was once used as a court where condemned prisoners were held before being hanged.

The story of Lady Onslow, who haunted the Archbishop's Palace after drowning in a fishpond in the grounds in 1718, was mentioned by Daniel Defoe in 'A Tour of the Whole Island of Great Britain' (1724-27), but there have not been any reported sightings of the ghost since the building became the Old Palace School.

A famous ghost story linked with Croydon Airport tells of a ghost who warned pilots of bad weather. He was supposed to be the ghost of a Dutch pilot who took off from the airport in 1930 but soon hit a wall of fog and died when his plane crashed. Several weeks later, an Imperial Airways pilot who had been a friend of the dead Dutchman was about to take off when he heard a voice warning him not to continue with the flight, because bad weather was fast approaching. He turned round and caught a quick glimpse of the figure of the Dutch pilot, which then disappeared. He cancelled the flight, and shortly afterwards the airport was engulfed in thick fog.

The carriage sheds at the old British Rail station at Addiscombe, which was demolished in 2001, were said to be haunted by the ghost of a train driver who was killed on the line in the early 20th century. It was said that trains were heard moving in the sheds at night. Sightings were also reported of a blurred, shadowy figure near the No 4 sidings, where a number of staff had been killed when a hot-water boiler exploded.

Grecian Villa on Beulah Hill in Upper Norwood is said to be haunted by 'Old Pottie' (Daniel Philpott), who had been a former stable-hand at the villa. The story goes that he looked at his reflection in a mirror in the house before committing suicide by hanging himself from a balcony because of his gambling debts. His reflection is supposed to be glimpsed occasionally in the mirror.

CROYDON MISCELLANY

The town of Croydon originally grew up around the parish church to the west of the present market place, but its economic centre developed further east towards the London road, where the market place was laid out to take advantage of the commercial traffic. The town grew to become one of a ring of corn and produce markets fringing London and supplying the capital's insatiable appetite.

The manor of Croydon was held by the Archbishop of Canterbury at the time of the Domesday Book, and the archbishopric built one of its palaces in the town, whose chief glory is the Great Hall which was built in the 1380s and altered in the 1440s. By the late 18th century the palace building had become dilapidated and was sold by the archbishopric. The buildings of what is now known as the Old Palace are still in use as the Old Palace School.

Croydon's medieval St John's Church was almost destroyed in a fire in 1867. All but the 15th-century west tower and south porch was rebuilt by the architect Sir George Gilbert Scott. Its association with the medieval Archbishop's Palace nearby accounts for its size, for the archbishops paid for its construction and six were buried inside it, including John Whitgift, whose alabaster effigy survived the fire.

ST JOHN'S CHURCH
c1955 C201048

THE WHITGIFT HOSPITAL OF THE HOLY TRINITY c1955 C201034

The Archbishops of Canterbury took a keen interest in the town, especially John Whitgift, archbishop from 1583 to 1604. He founded the almshouses, or Hospital of the Holy Trinity, at the junction of George Street, High Street, North End and Crown Hill, which were erected between 1596 and 1599. The Hospital provided almshouses for sixteen men and sixteen women in rooms grouped around a grass quadrangle. Archbishop Whitgift also established the Whitgift School, whose Master's House, just off George Street, was demolished in 1897; the almshouses themselves were saved from demolition a few years later after local protests against the plan, and they still stand in Croydon today, a remarkable survival in the centre of a town that was so keen to modernise.

Photograph C201040, below, shows the Whitgift Middle School. The large ecclesiastical-style tower was the centrepiece of the west range, originally designed by Sir Arthur Blomfield in 1869 for a Victorian revival of Archbishop Whitgift's grammar school which had first opened in 1600. The Grammar School moved in 1931 to new buildings at Haling Park in South Croydon and Whitgift Middle School moved in; it was renamed the Trinity School of John Whitgift in 1954 to avoid confusion with the main Whitgift School. In 1965 the school moved out to Shirley and the buildings were demolished; their site and the 12 acres of playing fields were redeveloped for a vast covered shopping mall and a tower block of offices, Rothschild House. As a gesture to the past, this vast complex was named the Whitgift Centre.

WHITGIFT MIDDLE SCHOOL c1950 C201040

THE TOWN HALL c1965 C201150

The foundation stone of the current Town Hall (Croydon's third) on Katharine Street was laid in 1892. The Town Hall was built on the station site of a branch line that ran the short distance from East Croydon Station to the back of the High Street, which had closed in 1890 (in fact, the Town Hall gardens preserve part of its cutting). This proud building with its tall tower is still the focus of the town.

In 1848 the Public Health Act provided powers for the setting up of local health boards, and Croydon was one of the first to do so. The Board's report on sanitary conditions in the town painted a picture of open privies discharging into water courses, rubbish and excrement thrown into public drains, tainted wells next to privies, drinking water polluted, frequent flooding, and churchyards with coffins buried one upon the other to within inches of the surface. The Board set about improving things: the streams and runnels disappeared, good drains were laid and a clean water supply provided. The most notable evidence of this is the old Waterworks building behind Surrey Street. The Board bought and re-erected the West Croydon Engine House of the Croydon Atmospheric Railway, which ran from Forest Hill to West Croydon from 1845 to 1847. The date '1851' records this rebuild. The taller battlemented 'castle' was added in 1867.

Several notable names from popular music were born or brought up in Croydon, including Adam Ant, the original members of the rock group The Damned, and the late singer/songwriter Kirsty MacColl.

SURREY STREET c1955 C201094

On the left of photograph C201094, above, is the former gaol, built in 1803. It was later converted to a warehouse and shop before being demolished in the 1950s.

The face of Croydon changed dramatically after the passing of the Croydon Corporation Act of 1956. The town was well placed for expansion because of its proximity to London, with excellent rail links, and with low office rentals. New office blocks rose up, many with a design brief to enclose as much space as high as possible. However, the interesting feature of Croydon is that much of its Victorian and pre-First World War heritage survived the architectural onslaught, partly because the focus of the great rebuild was parallel to the town's streets. Away from the commercial centre small-scale houses survive, and the council, since 1965 the London Borough of Croydon, continues to improve the town, and encourages the restoration of historic buildings.

Photograph C201145, below, shows Surrey House, on the left, and the Meat Market beyond, which has now replaced the former gaol seen in photograph C201094, opposite. By the Victorian period this area had become a slum with a warren of squalid lanes. The Croydon Improvement Act of 1890 cleared away the slums of the market area as well as providing for the road widening, and near the telephone box a plaque commemorates the widening of the High Street under Mayor Eldridge in 1896.

SURREY STREET, THE MARKET c1965 C201145

HIGH STREET c1965 C201137

The Davis Theatre which formerly stood in the High Street was vast; it opened in 1928 and had over 3,700 seats. On 14 January 1944, during the Second World War, a German bomb dropped by a plane fell through the roof of the Davis Theatre whilst 2,000 people were watching a film. Although seven people were killed and many were injured, luckily the bomb failed to explode, resulting in far fewer casualties than might have otherwise been the case. One of the most momentous occasions in the history of the Davis Theatre was when it hosted a performance by the renowned Russian Bolshoi Ballet. People queued for days for a ticket, in lines that stretched as far as East Croydon station. On 2 June 1953 a capacity audience watched the coronation of Queen Elizabeth II live on a 24ft-wide television screen that had been specially installed for the occasion. The Davis Theatre closed in May 1959 and a few months later it was demolished. The theatre can be seen standing in photograph C201090 on pages 18-19, and photograph C201137, above, shows the site in the course of being redeveloped; the theatre's place was taken by Davis House.

The first person to own a car in Croydon is thought to have been a Mr D P Roberts; he was a chemist and dealer in photographic and optical goods, whose business premises was at 120 North End (where Marks & Spencer now stands). He bought his car in October 1898, and used it to deliver goods to customers.

The recent revival of the tram network in Croydon is an exciting development. The new trams started running in 1999 and represent a survival of the system that ran from Edwardian times until 1951, when they were powered by overhead electric wires carried on elegant standards or, as seen in photograph C201015, below, on cables attached to buildings on each side of the road.

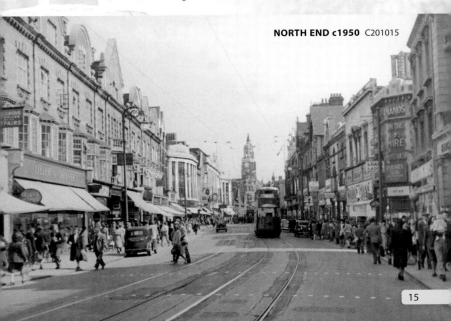

NORTH END c1950 C201015

NORTH END c1955 C201039

The first stretch of North End used to be dominated by two department stores, Kennard's and Allders. Kennard's, on the left of photograph C201039 (above) was demolished to make way for the Drummond Centre, a shopping centre and a Debenhams store. The rooftop of Kennard's was used for children's activities and was known as the 'Playground in the Sky'. To encourage customers to visit, the store even had its own zoo in the 1950s; this mainly consisted of different monkeys in cages and parrots and pet animals such as rabbits and guinea pigs, but there was also a whale on display at one time.

Recorded on a headstone in Croydon cemetery:
Poems and epitaphs are but stuff,
Here lies Bob Barras and that's enough.

At one time a great trade in charcoal was carried on in Croydon, occasioning poets to speak of 'Croydon clothed in black'.

The building housing Horne's men's shop in photograph C201076, below, still survives, and is dated 1910. It is in an unusual late Arts and Crafts style, worthy of closer examination for its judicious use of stone, decoration and design elements, which combine to produce an austere but highly creative version of Tudor architecture.

NORTH END c1960 C201076

Catherine Gowers Kettle was Croydon's first female mayor, elected
in 1961. A tragic event which occurred during Mayor Kettle's year
in office was the air disaster in Norway when an aircraft carrying
a group of schoolboys and teachers from Lanfranc Secondary
Modern School (now the Archbishop Lanfranc School in Mitcham

HIGH STREET c1955 C201090

Road, Thornton Heath) crashed into a hillside near Stavanger on 9 August 1961. The group from the school were heading for a holiday in the Norwegian highlands, but 34 boys and two teachers were killed. Mayor Kettle visited the scene of the crash and helped to forge strong bonds between the people of Croydon and Stavanger.

SHIRLEY, THE WINDMILL c1965 S556064

Shirley Windmill in Postmill Close is over 150 years old, and was originally built by Richard Alwen in 1854. Shirley Mill became uneconomic and was closed in 1893. It rapidly deteriorated and was twice struck by lightning, in 1899 and 1906. There were restoration attempts in 1927 and 1951 and the mill was nearly demolished when John Ruskin Grammar School was built in 1955, but was saved by strong public support. The mill has now been restored and is open to visitors, complete with touch-screen interactive displays, information panels and hands-on activities which make a visit there both informative, educational and fun.

One of the scoundrels of Croydon's history is its first mayor, elected in 1883, the disgraced MP Jabez Spencer Balfour. He lived in some style in Wellesley House in South Croydon (demolished in the 1950s), and was a colourful and high-profile character who was nicknamed Mr Croydon because of his various activities in the borough as a businessman, politician, philanthropist, and temperance campaigner. However, his charming manner concealed the fact that he was also a liar, adulterer and cheat. Balfour was the founder of the Liberator Building Society, which collapsed after extravagant malpractice in 1892, leaving thousands of people defrauded of their money and facing destitution. Balfour fled to Argentina, scandalously accompanied by his young female ward. He was eventually extradited and brought back to England where he was tried and sentenced to fourteen years' imprisonment, after which his portrait was removed from the council chamber in Croydon's Town Hall. For some time after the fall of the Liberator Building Society Balfour was the most notorious man in the country, and effigies of him were burnt on Bonfire Night.

The first car to be manufactured from scratch in Croydon was the 1902 Bradbury Voiturette, designed, built and marketed by Bradbury Bros. Six more 'Croydon' cars followed over the next three years, the Firefly, the Imperial, the Emerald, the General, the Weller and the Brotherhood. The most famous car producing company associated with Croydon is Trojan Limited, which was founded by Leslie Hounsfield in Purley Way, Croydon. The company began with simple two-stroke vehicles, and in the 1950s became the first to fit diesel engines into small vans. Trojan Ltd produced cars and especially delivery vans until 1964. Around 1960 the Trojan factory was sold to Peter Agg, who assembled Lambretta scooters for the English market. In 1962 the right to manufacture the Heinkel microcar was acquired, and these were also made at Croydon. In 1962 Trojan acquired the Elva sports car business and started to make the Mk IV Elva Courier, which in turn led on to the manufacturing of McLaren racing cars at Croydon until vehicle production finally ceased in the early 1970s. The first car made by Trojan is now owned by The Trojan Museum Trust, which has been formed in a bid to establish a museum devoted to the cars, vans and machinery made by Trojan Ltd. For more information, visit the Trust's website: www.trojanmuseumtrust.org

The Census returns for Croydon over the last 200 years make interesting reading. In 1801 the population of Croydon was 6,742; by 1901 it had risen to 141,918 and by 2001 it was 330,688. In 1851 125 babies in every 1,000 live births died before the age of one; by 1911 the number had reduced to 106 deaths in every 1,000 live births, and by 2001 the number was 7 in every 1,000.

SHIRLEY, ST JOHN'S PARISH CHURCH
c1955 S556021

SURREY STREET c1955 C201094x

Until slum clearance and new town developments provided inside
sanitation for all, public baths served those whose home ablutions
were confined to tin baths and outside toilets. In the early 1950s, one
in three homes still lacked an inside bathroom. The sign for Croydon's
public baths can be seen in photograph C201094x, above.

An old folk rhyme shows that Croydon has long been famous
for the beauty of its women:

'Sutton for good mutton,
Cheam for juicy beef,
Croydon for a pretty girl,
And Mitcham for a thief'.

Immediately east of Suffolk House was St Matthew's Church,
designed by Blomfield and built in 1866. It still survived in 1965,
when photograph C201249 (below) was taken, a forlorn piece of the
past amid the brave new world of Croydon. It lost its churchyard to
the dual carriageway; then, with few people living in the centre of
town, it was eventually closed and demolished. It is commemorated
in the name of the 1980s seven-storey tower, St Matthew's House.

ST MATTHEW'S CHURCH c1965 C201249

25

The Kennard's department store was renowned for its extravagant and bizarre selling techniques to pull in the customers; the store's manager Robert Driscoll would have chimpanzees dressed in suits and other circus animals on display to entertain and promote

the goods. One of his publicity stunts to advertise a 'jumbo sale' was to have two elephants at each side of North End to attract customers' attention, which caused chaos by blocking the passage of the trams.

THE TOWN HALL GARDENS c1950 C201011

SHIRLEY, THE TEA HOUSE c1960 S556034

Croydon has the unfortunate honour of holding two sad 'firsts' in motoring history. In 1896 a Croydon resident, Bridget Driscoll, became the road casualty in Britain when she was knocked down and killed near the Crystal Palace by an automobile that was being used to give demonstration rides. By a strange coincidence, in February 1898 Croydon became the location of the first death in the country resulting from a car accident, when Henry Lindfield died in Croydon General Hospital after the car in which he and his son were travelling crashed at Russell Hill, Purley.

A Croydon firm that became known internationally was Gillett and Johnston, clock-makers and bell-founders. Their clocks and bells were used not only in parish churches and public buildings in Britain, but also in well-known landmarks all over the world. William Gillett's business, based first in Whitehorse Road and then Union Road, was originally an important clock-making foundry, and by 1868 was one of the first steam-powered clock factories in the world; the business expanded to include bell-founding in 1877, when Arthur Johnston became a partner. More than 14,000 town hall clocks were made by the firm between 1844 and 1950. William Johnston's son Cyril took over the business after his father's death in 1916, and is credited with rediscovering the art of bell tuning, a skill which had been lost for more than 200 years, and Gillett and Johnston became known all over the world for the quality of their bells and carillons. One of the firm's contracts was the 72-bell carillon that was made for John Rockefeller Junior in New York, the largest in the world. The firm also recast London's famous Bow Bells in 1933. Cyril Johnston was awarded the OBE just before his death in 1950, and a letter to a newspaper at the time paid a moving tribute to his achievements: 'The bells that he has made are sounding melodiously in America and Canada, and elsewhere, when you and I are in bed and asleep. They are ringing here, there and everywhere in England while we are at work. They will go on ringing through the centuries, for there is no limit to the life of a bell'. The bell foundry in Union Road closed in the 1950s, but the clock tower of the foundry remained a famous Croydon landmark until it was demolished in 1997.

One of the greatest figures of the Victorian age was the poet, artist, critic, social revolutionary and conservationist John Ruskin (1819-1900). He spent much of his childhood in Croydon, which was the home of his mother's family, and his parents are buried in Shirley. The John Ruskin Grammar School in Croydon was named after him, and was renamed the John Ruskin High School in 1971. The school was demolished in 1991 to make way for a new housing development, and the upper forms were relocated to a Sixth Form College in Selsdon; the connection is retained in the name, John Ruskin College.

A famous name in Croydon's history is that of Samuel Coleridge-Taylor, the acclaimed black composer who was brought up in the town. He was born in Holborn in London in 1875; his mother was English and his father was a doctor from Sierra Leone in West Africa. Samuel's father tried to set up practice in England, but found it impossible to overcome the racial prejudice he encountered, and returned to Sierra Leone; the one-year-old Samuel and his mother then moved to Waddon. Samuel studied violin with a local musician, and his musical talent was encouraged by Colonel Herbert Walters, who belonged to the church choir in which the boy sang. Colonel Walters obtained an admission interview for Samuel at the Royal College of Music which led to his enrolment as a violin student in 1890, but two years later he switched to composition, and soon began to make a name for himself. The turning point in his musical career came in 1898, when he was 23, when Sir Edward Elgar asked him to compose a piece for the Three Choirs Festival; this was his 'Ballade in A Minor', which was a critical and popular success. Samuel Coleridge-Taylor died tragically young, at the age of 37, from pneumonia. He is remembered in Croydon by having a youth centre, a road and a school named after him, and there is a plaque commemorating his achievements at 30 Dagnall Park, Selhurst, where he lived.

THE TOWN HALL GARDENS c1950 C201013

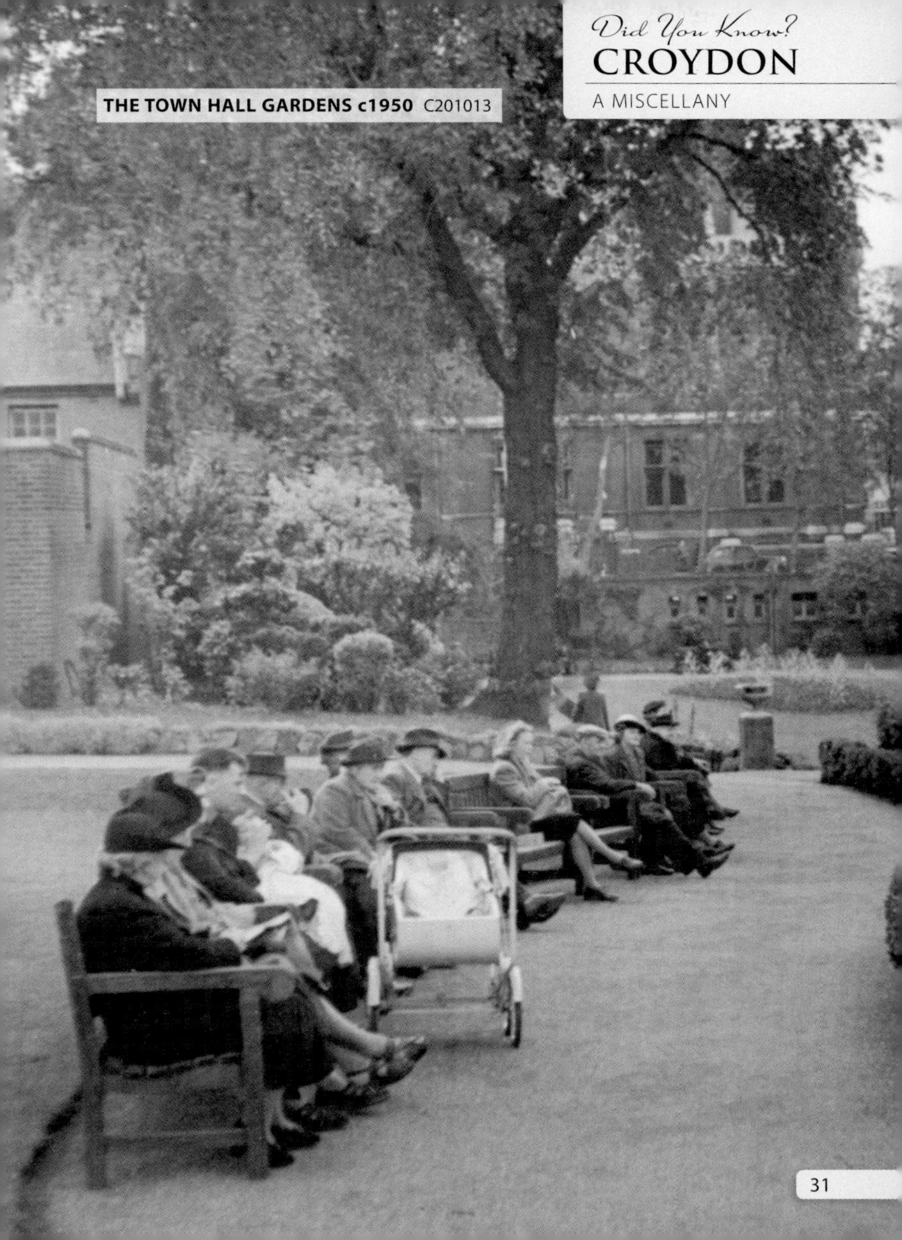

SHIRLEY, SHIRLEY ROAD c1955 S556006

During the First World War, nine people in Croydon were killed and a further fifteen were injured when the town was attacked by Germany's newest weapon, the Zeppelin airship, on the night of 13 October 1915. Eighteen 'pudding bombs' were dropped from the Zeppelin over the town centre, and the attack is described in 'Croydon and the Great War' by W C Berwick: 'A flash from the sky, a sudden illumination of the whole neighbourhood, a deafening explosion and violent tremors of the ground showed that the German invaders had actually reached Croydon. Explosions followed in rapid and terrifying succession as the Zeppelin crossed over Addiscombe, passed south and east of the London Brighton railway line and then throbbed away towards Woolwich'. The reason for the ferocious attack is not known, but it is possible that the target was the munitions factory at the corner of Cherry Orchard Road, or perhaps the network of railway lines at East Croydon, both of which were narrowly missed by the bombs.

The Croydon Canal was authorised by an Act of Parliament in 1801, and ran for 9.5 miles (15 km) from Croydon via Forest Hill to the Grand Surrey Canal at New Cross in south London. It opened on 22 October 1809. The Croydon Canal linked with the Croydon, Merstham & Godstone Railway, which allowed the canal to be used to transport stone and lime from workings at Merstham, although the main cargo on the canal was timber. The canal had 28 locks, arranged in two flights, and was supplied with water from a reservoir constructed at South Norwood. The canal was not commercially successful and was closed in 1836.

THE FLYOVER c1969 C201289

GEORGE STREET c1955 C201043

THE NEW (WHITGIFT) SHOPPING CENTRE c1970 C201270

There was great excitement in Croydon in January 1927 when a group of Sioux warriors visited the town. The streets were lined with crowds of people who had come to watch the Native Americans leave a train at Thornton Heath and ride into Croydon on horseback, where they were greeted by the mayor and given a civic reception. Local newspapers covered the story and no one was in any doubt that the exotic warriors were the genuine article. However, it later transpired that the whole event was a hoax, and the 'Sioux braves' were actually unemployed local men dressed up in war paint, costumes and feathered war bonnets. It is believed that the whole thing was a publicity stunt planned by the Kennard's store and the Hippodrome cinema, as it coincided with the showing there of the film 'The Vanishing Race', about what were then referred to as Red Indians.

Although the bell-foundry of the famous Croydon firm of Gillett and Johnston in Union Road is no more, the clock-making side of the business still thrives in smaller premises in Selsdon Road, South Croydon. Croydon landmarks such as the Clock Tower on Katharine Street and the Purley Street clock were created and are maintained by the company, which still supplies clocks all over the world.

LONDON ROAD c1960 C201123

At the beginning of the 19th century Croydon became the terminus of the pioneering horse-drawn Surrey Iron Railway from Wandsworth, which was Britain's first complete railway to be publicly subscribed by Act of Parliament. It was opened in 1803 and terminated at what is now Reeves Corner; in 1805 it was extended to Merstham and was known as the Croydon, Merstham & Godstone Railway. The railway was designed to carry bulk freight and followed a nine-mile route, serving the factories and mills of the valley of the River Wandle and the quarries near Godstone and Merstham. The horse-drawn railway was closed by the middle of the 19th century, unable to compete against steam locomotives.

Thousands of homes in Croydon were destroyed or damaged by air raids during the Second World War, and more than 750 civilians were killed. Most of the damage was caused during the period of V-1 'doodlebug' attacks in the summer of 1944, when Croydon received more 'doodlebug' hits than any other London Borough. The V-1s (and later the V-2s) were unmanned flying missiles that were fired across the Channel from France. They were nicknamed 'doodlebugs' because of the droning noise they made, which ceased when they were about to detonate; when the droning noise stopped, people had fifteen seconds to escape from the blast that followed. Many people remember the doodlebug attacks as being one of the most terrifying aspects of the war.

CHURCH STREET c1965 C201201

HIGH STREET c1955 C201052

NORTH END c1950 C201018

Charles Darwin is famous for his groundbreaking work on evolution, 'The Origin of Species', but a Croydon man, the naturalist Alfred Russel Wallace (1823-1913), who lived at 44 St Peter's Road, was also proposing a theory of evolution by natural selection at the same time, and this prompted Charles Darwin to publicise his own theory somewhat earlier than he had planned. The theory of evolution, which cast doubt on the story of creation as outlined in the Bible, was highly unpopular in the 19th century with many church leaders, and in an interview published after his death in 1913 Wallace said: 'Truth is born into this world only with pangs and tribulations, and every fresh truth is received unwillingly. To expect the world to receive a new truth, or even an old truth, without challenging it, is to look for one of those miracles which do not occur'.

One of the most interesting people in Croydon's story is Charles Burgess Fry, born on 25 April 1872 at 5 Edinburgh Villas (now 144 St James's Road). Fry, popularly known as 'CB', was not only possibly the greatest all-round sportsman of all time, but is also famous for a variety of other achievements. He is best remembered in his sporting career as a highly successful cricketer who played for Surrey, Sussex and Hampshire, and who captained England without ever losing a Test, but he was also a gifted soccer player who reached the FA Cup final playing for Southampton, and a rugby player for Oxford, Blackheath and the Barbarians. He also equalled the world long-jump record in 1892. Away from sport, he became a novelist and a successful journalist and came very close to becoming an MP.

LONDON ROAD c1950 C201027

NORTH END 1966 C201205

SPORTING CROYDON

Crystal Palace FC have been a dominant force in sport in the Croydon area for most of the last 100 years. The club, so-called because their first ground was built on the site of the Crystal Palace in Sydenham, has been notable for its regular movement between divisions. For instance, Palace hold the dubious record of being the only club to be relegated from the Premier League on four occasions. In recent times the club's manager, Iain Dowie, coined the word 'Bouncebackability', meaning the ability to recover, or bounce back, from a failure. It was perhaps apt that a Palace manager should come up with such a word, since it seems to sum the club up perfectly.

One of the best-known sportsmen with strong Croydon connections is the footballer Ian Wright. Originally from Greenwich, he was spotted playing local football by Crystal Palace, who gave him his first professional contract. Among his many achievements in a distinguished career was winning the 'Golden Boot' as the top goal scorer in Division One during his first season at Arsenal. He is also the highest post-war goal scorer for Crystal Palace, and is Arsenal's second highest goal scorer. He played 33 times for England.

Croydon played an important part in the early development of cricket. Some of the very first reports of organised matches in the early 18th century are of matches played in the area. Among these are reports of two games between Croydon and London in July 1707, one of the matches probably being played at Duppas Hill in Croydon.

One of Croydon's better-known cricketers is Alan Butcher. Born in Croydon in 1954, he was a Wisden Cricketer of the Year in 1991, a year before his retirement. He played for England on one occasion. Alan once played against his son, the well-known England batsman Mark Butcher, in a Sunday League game at the Oval. This is surely a unique event in the modern game.

Croydon is home to one of Britain's most successful sporting families. The McKenzie family has produced a number of top boxers, including Clinton, a British Light-Welterweight Champion and Olympic silver medallist, and Winston, a national amateur boxing champion. The most famous member though, is Duke, who has won world boxing titles at three different weights, an extraordinary achievement. Another family member, Leon, has played Premiership football for Norwich City.

QUIZ QUESTIONS

Answers on page 48.

1. Whose advertising slogan was 'We Entertain To Sell and We Sell To Entertain'?

2. What is the origin of the name 'Croydon'?

3. What is the link between Croydon and Sherlock Holmes?

4. Part of the Fairfield Halls is named the Ashcroft Theatre - which former Croydon resident does this commemorate?

5. Which were the two most popular films to be shown during the lifetime of the Davis Theatre in the High Street, which was demolished in 1959?

6. Which supermodel is a Croydon girl?

7. What is the link between Croydon and fairies?

8. The words 'To make your children capable of honesty is the beginning of education' were written by which famous person with Croydon connections?

9. What is the best-known work of Samuel Coleridge-Taylor, the acclaimed black composer who was brought up in the town?

10. One of the most famous film directors in cinematic history was born in Croydon in 1908, but his parents, who were strict Quakers, actually forbade him from visiting the cinema whilst he was a boy, as they believed that such places were 'dens of vice'. Who was he, and can you name some of his most successful films?

GEORGE STREET c1965 C201199

RECIPE

SPRING VEGETABLES IN SAUCE
*In the 19th century market gardening was particularly important around
Thornton Heath, providing fruit and vegetables for the rapidly growing
population of the area and also for the London markets.*

Ingredients

50g/2oz butter
8 small young carrots,
scraped
16 small new potatoes,
scraped
16 spring onions, peeled and
trimmed
Bouquet of thyme, parsley
and mint sprigs
1 tablespoonful plain flour

300ml/½ pint vegetable or
chicken stock
150ml/¼ pint dry white wine
225g/8oz shelled peas, fresh
or frozen
225g/8oz shelled broad
beans, fresh or frozen
1 teaspoonful salt
1 teaspoonful caster sugar
1 tablespoonful double
cream

Melt the butter in a saucepan, add the carrots, potatoes and spring
onions, and toss well to coat in the melted butter. Add the herbs.
Sprinkle in the flour, then gradually stir in the stock and wine. Cover
and simmer for 10 minutes. Stir in the peas and broad beans and
simmer for a further 10 minutes until all the vegetables are tender.
Remove from the heat and stir in the salt, sugar and cream. Transfer
to a heated serving dish and serve either as a vegetarian main course
garnished with croutons, or as an accompaniment to meat or fish.

WANDLE PARK c1950 C201055

Did You Know?
CROYDON
A MISCELLANY

RECIPE

SURREY LOVING CUP

Croydon is now the principal town of the London Borough of Croydon, but has its historic roots in Surrey. Use sparkling wine in this recipe for a refreshing summer drink, and champagne for a special occasion. This drink was traditionally served in a special two-handled 'Loving Cup' or glass.

Ingredients

2 large fresh lemons
110g/4oz sugar cubes
300ml/10fl oz hot water
300ml/10fl oz cold water
Half a bottle of Madeira wine
150ml/5fl oz brandy

1 bottle of champagne or sparkling white wine, chilled
Fresh lemon balm leaves - for decoration
Fresh borage flowers - for decoration

Rub the lemons with the sugar cubes so that they absorb the lemon oil, then place the cubes in a large heatproof jug and pour the hot water over them. Stir until all the sugar is dissolved, then leave to cool.

Peel the lemons very finely, and add the peel to the sugar mixture. Remove the white pith from the lemons and cut them into very thin slices, removing the pips. Add the sliced lemons, the cold water, the Madeira wine and the brandy to the sugar and lemon liquid, cover and chill in the fridge for at least one hour.

Remove the lemon peel just before serving, and pour the liquid into a large glass jug or punchbowl. Add the champagne or sparkling wine, and decorate with the lemon balm leaves and borage flowers.

Did You Know?
CROYDON
A MISCELLANY

QUIZ ANSWERS

1. Kennard's, the department store in North End, now replaced by the Drummond Centre. The colourful history of this major Croydon attraction has been vividly chronicled by the historian Vivien Lovett in 'Kennard's of Croydon: The Store that Entertained to Sell'.

2. There are several interpretations of the name of Croydon. One possibility is that the name comes from the Anglo-Saxon words 'croeas deanas', which means 'the crocus valley', which suggests that it may have been where the valuable saffron crocus grew. Another theory is that the name comes from the Old French 'croie dune', meaning 'chalk hill', describing Croydon's position on the North Downs. A third possibility is that it comes from the Anglo-Saxon 'crogdaen', which means 'crooked valley'.

3. The author Sir Arthur Conan Doyle (1859-1930), creator of Sherlock Holmes, lived at 12 Tennison Road, South Norwood between 1891 and 1894.

4. The Ashcroft Theatre commemorates a famous name in theatrical history - the actress Dame Peggy Ashcroft (1907-1991), who was born in Croydon and lived in George Street as a child.

5. The two most successful films to be shown at the Davis Theatre were Disney's 'Snow White and the Seven Dwarfs' and 'The Wicked Lady', starring Margaret Lockwood.

6. The supermodel Kate Moss, who was born and raised in Croydon.

7. The illustrator and artist Cicely Mary Barker (1895-1973), who created the famous Flower Fairies books, was born in Croydon. She studied at Croydon School of Art and continued to live in the town, often using local children as models for the fairies in her paintings.

8. John Ruskin, after whom the John Ruskin Grammar School, later the John Ruskin High School, was named. He had family connections with Croydon, and spent much of his childhood in the town.

9. The best-known work of the composer Samuel Coleridge-Taylor is 'Hiawatha's Wedding'.

10. David Lean, who directed some of the most acclaimed epics in film history, including 'Brief Encounter', 'Great Expectations', 'Oliver Twist', 'The Bridge On The River Kwai', 'Lawrence of Arabia', 'Dr Zhivago', and 'A Passage To India'. Born in 1908, David Lean lived with his parents, Frank and Helena Lean, and his brother first at 38 Blenheim Crescent and later 3 Warham Road in South Croydon, and the family moved to 97 Park Lane in 1921. His first - secret - visit to a cinema was at the age of thirteen, and he continued to sneak away to the cinema at regular intervals, captivated by the world of film. His mother knew about the visits but kept them a secret from his father, and David Lean went on to become a director whose films won a total of 26 Oscars. He said in later life that one of his greatest regrets was that he had never been able to persuade his father to watch one of his films.

ADDISCOMBE, SHIRLEY ROAD, THE PARADE c1965 A267010

FRANCIS FRITH

PIONEER VICTORIAN PHOTOGRAPHER

Francis Frith, founder of the world-famous photographic archive, was a complex and multi-talented man. A devout Quaker and a highly successful Victorian businessman, he was philosophical by nature and pioneering in outlook. By 1855 he had already established a wholesale grocery business in Liverpool, and sold it for the astonishing sum of £200,000, which is the equivalent today of over £15,000,000. Now in his thirties, and captivated by the new science of photography, Frith set out on a series of pioneering journeys up the Nile and to the Near East.

INTRIGUE AND EXPLORATION

He was the first photographer to venture beyond the sixth cataract of the Nile. Africa was still the mysterious 'Dark Continent', and Stanley and Livingstone's historic meeting was a decade into the future. The conditions for picture taking confound belief. He laboured for hours in his wicker dark-room in the sweltering heat of the desert, while the volatile chemicals fizzed dangerously in their trays. Back in London he exhibited his photographs and was 'rapturously cheered' by members of the Royal Society. His reputation as a photographer was made overnight.

VENTURE OF A LIFE-TIME

By the 1870s the railways had threaded their way across the country, and Bank Holidays and half-day Saturdays had been made obligatory by Act of Parliament. All of a sudden the working man and his family were able to enjoy days out, take holidays, and see a little more of the world.

With typical business acumen, Francis Frith foresaw that these new tourists would enjoy having souvenirs to commemorate their days out. For the next thirty years he travelled the country by train and by pony and trap, producing fine photographs of seaside resorts and beauty spots that were keenly bought by millions of Victorians. These prints were painstakingly pasted into family albums and pored over during the dark nights of winter, rekindling precious memories of summer excursions. Frith's studio was soon supplying retail shops all over the country, and by 1890 F Frith & Co had become the greatest specialist photographic publishing company in the world, with over 2,000 sales outlets, and pioneered the picture postcard.

FRANCIS FRITH'S LEGACY

Francis Frith had died in 1898 at his villa in Cannes, his great project still growing. By 1970 the archive he created contained over a third of a million pictures showing 7,000 British towns and villages.

Frith's legacy to us today is of immense significance and value, for the magnificent archive of evocative photographs he created provides a unique record of change in the cities, towns and villages throughout Britain over a century and more. Frith and his fellow studio photographers revisited locations many times down the years to update their views, compiling for us an enthralling and colourful pageant of British life and character.

We are fortunate that Frith was dedicated to recording the minutiae of everyday life. For it is this sheer wealth of visual data, the painstaking chronicle of changes in dress, transport, street layouts, buildings, housing and landscape that captivates us so much today, offering us a powerful link with the past and with the lives of our ancestors.

Computers have now made it possible for Frith's many thousands of images to be accessed almost instantly. The archive offers every one of us an opportunity to examine the places where we and our families have lived and worked down the years. Its images, depicting our shared past, are now bringing pleasure and enlightenment to millions around the world a century and more after his death.

For further information visit: www.francisfrith.com

INTERIOR DECORATION

Frith's photographs can be seen framed and as giant wall murals in thousands of pubs, restaurants, hotels, banks, retail stores and other public buildings throughout Britain. These provide interesting and attractive décor, generating strong local interest and acting as a powerful reminder of gentler days in our increasingly busy and frenetic world.

FRITH PRODUCTS

All Frith photographs are available as prints and posters in a variety of different sizes and styles. In the UK we also offer a range of other gift and stationery products illustrated with Frith photographs, although many of these are not available for delivery outside the UK – see our web site for more information on the products available for delivery in your country.

THE INTERNET

Over 100,000 photographs of Britain can be viewed and purchased on the Frith web site. The web site also includes memories and reminiscences contributed by our customers, who have personal knowledge of localities and of the people and properties depicted in Frith photographs. If you wish to learn more about a specific town or village you may find these reminiscences fascinating to browse. Why not add your own comments if you think they would be of interest to others? See **www.francisfrith.com**

PLEASE HELP US BRING FRITH'S PHOTOGRAPHS TO LIFE

Our authors do their best to recount the history of the places they write about. They give insights into how particular towns and villages developed, they describe the architecture of streets and buildings, and they discuss the lives of famous people who lived there. But however knowledgeable our authors are, the story they tell is necessarily incomplete.

Frith's photographs are so much more than plain historical documents. They are living proofs of the flow of human life down the generations. They show real people at real moments in history; and each of those people is the son or daughter of someone, the brother or sister, aunt or uncle, grandfather or grandmother of someone else. All of them lived, worked and played in the streets depicted in Frith's photographs.

We would be grateful if you would give us your insights into the places shown in our photographs: the streets and buildings, the shops, businesses and industries. Post your memories of life in those streets on the Frith website: what it was like growing up there, who ran the local shop and what shopping was like years ago; if your workplace is shown tell us about your working day and what the building is used for now. Read other visitors' memories and reconnect with your shared local history and heritage. With your help more and more Frith photographs can be brought to life, and vital memories preserved for posterity, and for the benefit of historians in the future.

Wherever possible, we will try to include some of your comments in future editions of our books. Moreover, if you spot errors in dates, titles or other facts, please let us know, because our archive records are not always completely accurate—they rely on 140 years of human endeavour and hand-compiled records. You can email us using the contact form on the website.

Thank you!

For further information, trade, or author enquiries
please contact us at the address below:

**The Francis Frith Collection, Frith's Barn, Teffont,
Salisbury, Wiltshire, England SP3 5QP.**
Tel: +44 (0)1722 716 376 Fax: +44 (0)1722 716 881
e-mail: sales@francisfrith.co.uk **www.francisfrith.com**